GRAVITY

by Robin Nelson

first step nonfiction

Lerner ... eapolis

Gravity is a **force.**

A force is a push or a pull.

Gravity pulls things and people to the ground.

Gravity pulls things down.

Gravity pulls leaves down.

Gravity pulls water down.

Gravity pulls apples down.

Gravity pulls a ball down.

Gravity pulls a roller
coaster down.

Gravity pulls a sled down.

Gravity pulls sand down.

Gravity pulls a **yo-yo** down.

Gravity pulls
sky divers down.

Gravity pulls rain down.

Gravity pulls me down.

Gravity is everywhere.

The Leaning Tower of Pisa

Galileo

Galileo

Long ago, a scientist named Galileo did an experiment with gravity. The story says that he went to the top of the Leaning Tower of Pisa and dropped two balls. One ball was heavy, and one was light. The two balls hit the ground at the same time. This showed that gravity pulls all objects to the ground at the same speed no matter what they weigh.

Gravity Facts

 Gravity pulls things toward the center of Earth.

 There is very little gravity in space. This is why astronauts float around in space.

 Your weight is the amount of force pulling you down to the ground.

 The Sun's gravity attracts the planets.

Earth's gravity draws the Moon toward Earth. Without it, the Moon would go flying into space.

 One story says that a scientist named Sir Isaac Newton first started thinking about gravity when an apple fell from a tree and hit him on the head.

Glossary

 force – a push or pull on an object

 gravity – a force that pulls things

 sky diver – someone who jumps from an airplane

 yo-yo – a toy that goes up and down on a string

Index

The photographs in this book are reproduced through the courtesy of: © Richard Cummins, cover, p. 10; Digital Vision Royalty Free, pp. 2, 22 (middle); Brand X Pictures, pp. 3, 22 (second from top); © Tom Stewart/CORBIS, p. 4; © Diane Meyer, p. 5; © Index Stock Imagery/David Davis, p. 6; © Brian Lawrence/SuperStock, p. 7; © Bonnie Sue, p. 8; PhotoDisc Royalty Free by Getty Images, pp. 9, 12, 14, 17, 22 (top and second from bottom); © Steven Graham Photography, p. 11; © Todd Strand/Independent Picture Service, pp. 13, 22 (bottom); © David Cavagnaro/ Visuals Unlimited, p.15; © Image Source Ltd., p. 16; Corbis Royalty Free, p. 18 (left); New York Public Library, p. 18 (right).

Lerner Publications Company
A division of Lerner Publishing Group
241 First Avenue North
Minneapolis, MN 55401 U.S.A.

Website address: www.lernerbooks.com

Library of Congress Cataloging-in-Publication Data

Nelson, Robin, 1971–
        Gravity / by Robin Nelson.
            p.   cm. — (First step nonfiction)
        Includes index.
        Summary: An introduction to gravity and its effects.
        ISBN: 0–8225–5133–0 (lib. bdg. : alk. paper)
        ISBN: 0–8225–5297–3 (pbk. : alk. paper)
        1. Gravity—Juvenile literature. [1. Gravity.] I. Title. II. Series.
    QC178.N45 2004
    531'.6—dc22   2003013884

Manufactured in the United States of America
1 2 3 4 5 6 – DP – 09 08 07 06 05 04